HISTORY
OF THE
GUTELIUS FAMILY

DESCENDANTS OF

Adam Frederick Gutelius

COMPILED BY

WILL B. GUTELIUS

BLUFFTON, INDIANA

1916

1811.   .   1893

1702692

DEDICATION
IN MEMORY OF
SARAH (SALLY) GUTELIUS GROVE.

The last surviving child of the family of Frederick A. and Anna Catherine Bistel Gutelius, who were parents of eleven sons and four daughters.

It was the writer's privilege to meet this saint in the fall of 1891, at Mifflinburg, Pa. In her then 80th year she knew of 443 descendants of Adam Frederick Gutelius. It is largely due her, that we are able to give the following history and this slight tribute to her memory is affectionately offered.

WILL B. GUTELIUS.

Bluffton, Wells County, Indiana.
June 1, 1916.

HISTORICAL

ADAM FREDERICK GUTELIUS.

The first of the name of which we have any record, was a Frenchman and was educated for an army surgeon, by the government under which he lived.

He was the father of John Peter Gutelius, who was the first GUTELIUS, to set his feet on American soil.

The date of his birth, death and history of his life, other than that of the above is unknown.

The descendants of Adam Frederick Gutelius cover a period of about 225 years and comprises eight generations.

JOHN PETER GUTELIUS.

Son of Adam Frederick Gutelius, was born in France, in the year 1708 and died at Manheim, Pennsylvania, September 29th, 1773, age 65 years. He came to the United States at an early, to us, an unknown date, but tradition says, that he sailed from Rotterdam, Holland on ship Nancy, (Thomas Compton, Master). He qualified at Philadelphia, Pa., August 31st, 1750. According to tradition 'tis said that he was a physician to the Queen of France and that he was banished from the country on account of marrying out of his station.

His wife's maiden name was Anna Maria Deitzler, she being of Holland descent. The earliest residence location known of the above ancestors was at Manheim, Lancaster County, Pennsylvania, located 10 miles northwest of Lancaster, Pa.

They are buried in the Reformed Cemetery at Manheim, Pa., the location of his grave, being the first one back of the old church

A monument is erected to his memory and the following inscription, in German, translated reads:

Here Rests in God
JOHN PETER GUTELIUS
An eminent Surgeon and Physician
Born —————————, 1708   Died: September 29th, 1773.

How many children were born to this union is not known, but a silent grave in the above cemetery, says one John Peter Gutelius, born in 1765. Another Frederick Adam Gutelius was born in 1766, who became the paternal ancestor of all the GUTELIUSES in the United States.

FREDERICK ADAM GUTELIUS.

Son of John Peter and Anna Maria Gutelius, was born in Lancaster County, Pennsylvania, December 26th, 1766, and died at Mifflinburg, Pa., May 30th, 1839, age 72 years, 5 months and 4 days.

He was united in marriage to Anna Catherine Bistel, August 31st, 1790, who was born April 2nd, 1773 and died May 11th, 1838, age 65 years 1 month and 9 days. They moved to Mifflinburg, Pa., located about 65 miles northwest of Harrisburg, Pa., about the year 1800, using one two-horse team for transporting the household goods, while the family followed on foot.

They resided at the northeast corner of 5th and Green Streets, the property now being owned by his great grandson, Frederick Gutelius.

He was a blacksmith by trade and then studied surveying.

In 1813 he was elected one of the county commissioners of the new county of Union, upon its organization and in 1814 was appointed Esquire by Governor Thomas McKean. He did much surveying and conveying

He was a member of the Reformed Church at Mifflinburg and for many years was treasurer and secretary of that church.

He and his wife are buried in the east end of the old cemetery, about 150 feet southwest of the old church.

They were parents of fifteen children, eleven sons and four daughters, as follows:

Elizabeth Gutelius, Born July 30th, 1791. Died———.

William Gutelius, Born October 17th, 1792. Died May 3rd., 1793.

William Gutelius, Born February 15th, 1794. Died February 10th, 1857.

Samuel Gutelius, Born October 22nd, 1795. Died July 9th, 1866.

John Frederick Gutelius, Born March 17th, 1797. Died February 13th, 1866.

John Peter Gutelius. Born November 21st, 1798. Died July 16th. 1871.

Annie Catherine Gutelius, Born July 25th 1800. Died March 23rd, 1884.

David Gutelius, Born January 3rd, 1802. Died —————————————— 1879.

Israel Gutelius, Born October 30th, 1803. Died —————————————— 1863.

Annie Maria Gutelius, Born March 17th, 1805. Died April 4th, 1805.

Henry Gutelius, Born May 27th. 1806. Died —————————————— 1879.

Andrew Gutelius, Born April 16th, 1808. Died September 5th. 1874.

Sarah Gutelius, Born January 4th, 1811. Died April 29th, 1892.

George Gutelius Born November 1st, 1812. Died April 27th, 1889.

Joseph Gutelius, Born November 4th, 1815. Died February 10th. 1866.

All the above children married and resided in Mifflinburg, Pa., with the exception of John Peter Gutelius. David Gutelius and Annie Catherine Gutelius, who emigrated to Ohio.

There was no race suicide with this generation. as they were all heads of large families. This fact no doubt accounts for no great wealth being accumulated by either.

In personal appearance they were tall, straight, rough boned, with the exception of a few who were stout.

Their education was in German, but they also acquired the English language.

This remarkable family was noted for patriotism and piety from its earliest existence. They were of a very religious temperment. of the Prostestant faith, baptized in their youth and received into the Reformed Church

There are more persons bearing the name of GU-TELIUS in Mifflinburg, Pa., than any other name. The present generations living now reside in almost' all parts of the United States, but especially the Eastern Middle and Western States. They are not only confined to the United States, but are to be found in foreign lands, serving our blessed Saviour. Jesus Christ.

ELIZABETH GUTELIUS.

Eldest child and daughter of Frederick A. and Anna Catherine Bistel Gutelius, was born July 30th, 1791. Died ————————.

She was united in marriage to Jacob Detrich. They are buried in the old cemetery at Mifflinburg, Pa.

Born to this union. five children:

John E. Detrich, born June 7th, ————, died January 31st, 1899.

Anna Catherine Detrich Clauser, born July 19th, 1814, died October 13th, 1861.

Eliza Detrich Beaver, born December 23rd 1818, died August 8th, 1896.

Sarah Magdolene Detrich Harter, born August 27th, 1820, died December 30th, 1892.

Jacob S. Detrich, born ———————, died in 1870.

John E. Detrich's parents died while he was a young man and he was reared and educated by his uncle, John Peter Gutelius. In 1839 he moved to Sparta, Ill., and established the Sparta Democrat. He was elected member of the Legislature in 1850, State Senate in 1852 and Legislature in 1858.

He was captain of Company "I." 22nd Illinois Regiment.

He was appointed Commission of Enrollment for the 12th Congressional District with headquarters at Alton, Ill. In 1869 was appointed Internal Revenue Collector of the above district.

In 1883 he was appointed to a position in the Pension Office at Washington, D. C., which position he resigned in 1898.

WILLIAM GUTELIUS.

Second child and first son of Frederick A. and Anna
Catherine Bistel Gutelius was born October 17th, 1792
and died May 3rd, 1793, age 6 months and 16 days.

WILLIAM GUTELIUS.

Third child and second son of Frederick A. and
Anna Catherine Bistel Gutelius, was born February 15th,
1794 and died February 10th, 1857, age 62 years, 11
months and 25 days.

He was a bachelor. He was very lame and made
his home with his brother, Joseph Gutelius. Had no
trade or profession. Member of the Reformed Church.
Buried at Mifflinburg, Pa.

SAMUEL GUTELIUS.

Fourth child and third son of Frederick A. and Anna Catherine Bistel Gutelius, was born at Manheim, Lancaster County. Pa., October 22nd, 1795, died at Lykens. Pa. July 9th, 1866, age 70 years, 8 months and 17 days.

He was united in marriage to Anna Mary Small of York, Pa.

His second marriage was to Harriet Amelia Pyle, February 22nd, 1838.

She was born in Lancaster County, Pa., May 13th. 1813, died in Pittsburgh, Pa., September 7th, 1892.

He was a prominent minister of the Reformed Church. having been pastor of churches at York, Pa., Hanover, Pa., Gettysburg. Pa. Baltimore, Md., Littlestown. Pa., Freeburg, Pa., and Lykens, Pa.

His name is on memorial windows of the churches at Gettysburg and Hanover.

Born to this latter union: eight children:

Mary Gutelius Moore. born March 27th, 1840. Address: 1921 Ritner St., Philadelphia, Pa.

Nevin Pyle Gutelius, born in 1842. Last address Lima, Peru.

Sarah Catherine Gutelius Durbin, born February 10th, 1845. Address 717 N. 6th St. Harrisburg, Pa.

Emma Gutelius Earhart, born August 28th, 1847. Address Oxford, Kas.

Edwin S. Gutelius, born August 28th, 1849. died April, 1912.

Harriet Amelia Gutelius Coath, born in 1851, died December ————, 1895.

Ella Passmore Gutelius Coslett, born in 1854. Address: New Philadelphia, Ohio.

William Henry Gutelius. born July 4th, 1860. Address 44-60 East 23rd St., New York City N. Y.

William H. Gutelius, Jr., son of William Henry Gutelius, has charge of the dental department of the Christian College at Canton, China.

JOHN FREDERICK GUTELIUS.

Fifth child and fourth son of Frederick A. and Anna Catherine Bistel Gutelius, was born March 17th, 1797 and died at Mifflinburg, Pa., February 13th, 1866, age 68 years, 10 months and 26 days.

He was united in marriage to Lydia Crotzer, June 6th 1822. She was born at Mifflinburg, Pa., May 10th, 1804 and died January 5th, 1894, age 89 years, 7 months and 25 days. He was a dyer and weaver by trade. They were members of the Reformed Church and are buried at Mifflinburg, Pa.

Born to this union, ten children:

Thomas O. Gutelius, born April 3rd, 1823, died December 9th, 1902.

William Gutelius, born November 6th, 1824, died

John Gutelius, born August 19th, 1826, died _____.

Anna Caroline Gutelius Shriner, born October 2nd, 1828, died December 2nd, 1898.

Catherine R. Gutelius Foust, born October 19th, 1830, died October 6th, 1908.

Jacob Gutelius, born November 4th, 1832, died June 6th, 1897.

Samuel G. Gutélius, born November 9th, 1834, died July 25th, 1895.

Charles H. Gutelius, born November 18th 1836, died December 8th, 1913.

Joseph Gutelius, born January 1st, 1842, killed on battle field at Gettysburg.

Mary Lydia Gutelius, born October 18th, 1845, living at Mifflinburg, Pa.

Frederick P. Gutelius, a son of Jacob Gutelius, graduated from Lafayette College, Pa., and later became chief engineer of the Canadian Pacific Railroad. Recently he was put in charge, by the Canadian Government, of its large system of government owned railroads. Boil down our own Interstate Commerce Commission into the man, continue the present powers and add to them the direct management of a large system of government owned roads and you will have a fair idea of his responsible position.

JOHANNAS (JOHN) PETER GUTELIUS.

Sixth child and fifth son of Frederick A. and Anna Catherine Eistel Gutelius, was born at Manheim, Lancaster County, Pennsylvania, November 21st, 1798. Baptised in Reformed Church March 2nd, 1799. Died July 16th, 1871, age 72 years, 7 months and 25 days. Buried in Fairview Cemetery, Bluffton, Indiana. He was named after his Grandfather John Peter Gutelius. He was Prothonotary of Union County, Pa., in 1840. Hatter by trade. Drygoods merchant at Columbus, Ohio and Pickrington, Ohio, also a grain buyer and owner of a grocery supply house at Carroll, Ohio. He was a member of Charity Lodge 144, Ancient York Masons of Milton, Northumberland County, Pa, being made a Master Mason April 24th, 1823.

He was united in marriage to Maria Arndt, March 18th, 1823, who was born at Lebanon, Pa., July 5th, 1800 and died July 2nd, 1836.

Born to this union, two children:

Susan Catherine Gutelius born November 4th, 1828 and died ——————, 1907.

Margaret Arndt Gutelius, born December 18th, 1832, and died May 4th, 1905.

His second wife's maiden name was Henrietta Turner, they being united in marriage January 8th, 1839. She was born March 27th, 1818 and died July 22nd, 1888. They moved to Ohio about the year 1841.

Born to this union, eight children:

Martha Jane Gutelius, born January 13th, 1840.

Henrietta Turner Gutelius, born June 25th, 1841, died April 20th 1842.

Henrietta L. Gutelius, born April 8th, 1843.

John Allen Gutelius, born January 20th, 1845, died February 11th, 1848.

William Allen Gutelius, born June 5th, 1848.

Mary Elizabeth Gutelius, born February 15th, 1850, died ————————, 1878.

Emma Maria Gutelius, born January 17th, 1852.

Thomas Holmes Gutelius, born May 8th 1856.

ANNA CATHERINE GUTELIUS.

Seventh child and second daughter of Frederick A. and Anna Catherine Bistel Gutelius, was born in Lancaster County, Pennsylvania, July 25th, 1800. Died March 23rd, 1884, age 83 years, 7 months and 28 days.

She was united in marriage to Peter Yearick, May 10th, 1818, by Rev. Henry Price at Mifflinburg, Pa.

He was born December 20th, 1797 and died in 1885, being past 88 years of age. In the spring of 1834 they moved to Ashland County (then Wayne County) Ohio. Moved to Johnson County, Iowa in 1855. Returned to Ashland. Ohio, in 1871 and moved to Findlay, Ohio in 1872

Born to this union, fourteen children:

Elvina Yearick Goodwin, born September 10th, 1820, died at Findlay, Ohio July 3rd, 1891.

Susanna Yearick, born October 27th, 1821, died at the age of 6 years.

Henry E. Yearick, born December 23rd, 1823, died at Washington, Iowa, in 1892.

Elizabeth Yearick Shutt, born December 11th, 1825 died at Ashland, Ohio, 1889.

Gutelius Israel Yearick, born August 11th, 1827, died at Ashland, Ohio, in 1900.

Anna Caroline Yearick, born February 19th, 1829. Living at Old Ladies' Home, Toledo, Ohio.

Frederick Emmanuel Yearick, born September 26th, 1830 died in Nebraska in 1910.

Catherine Yearick Switzer, born February 9th, 1832 Living at Iowa Soldier's Home, at Marshalltown, Iowa.

Rebecca Yearick. born September 3rd, 1834. died at the age of 17. at Ashland. O.

Dr. Samuel William Yearick, born September 2nd, 1836, died at Cedar Rapids, Iowa, in 1910.

Mary Ann Yearick Line. born March 24th. 1838. Living at Milford. Neb.

John A. Yearick, born April 14th, 1840. Living at Iowa City, Iowa.

Joseph Peter Yearick, born June 3rd, 1843, died at Toledo, O., in 1901.

Simon A. Yearick. born November 22nd, 1845. Living at Woodward. Okla.

Five sons of Catherine Gutelius Yearick, saw service in the Civil War:

Frederick Emmanuel Yearick, 8th Iowa Infantry.

Samuel William Yearick, 13th Iowa Infantry.

John A. Yearick. 28th Iowa Infantry.

Joseph Peter Yearick, a teamster.

Simon A. Yearick. 100 days service.

DAVID GUTELIUS.

Eighth child and sixth son of Frederick A. and Anna Catherine Bistel Gutelius, was born January 3rd, 1802 and died ———, 1879.

He was the father of four children:

Thomas Gutelius, living at Thornville, Ohio.

Theodore Gutelius.

John Gutelius.

Mollie Gutelius Long.

ISRAEL GUTELIUS.

Ninth child and seventh son of Frederick A. and Anna Catherine Bistel Gutelius, was born in East Buffalo Township. Union County, Pennsylvania, October 30th, 1803 and died in 1863.

He was united in marriage to Sarah Haus, who was

born at Trappe, Montgomery County Pennsylvania, in 1811 and died in 1888. He was elected Sheriff of Union County in 1840. Also editor and proprietor of the "Union Star," a weekly, published at New Berlin, Pa.

Born to this union, ten children:

Mrs. Louisa Gutelius Weiser, widow, living at East Greenville. Pa.

Mrs. Henrietta Gutelius Crouse. Deceased.

Mrs. Sarah Catherine Gutelius Byers. Deceased.

John Percival Gutelius, died in 1863.

Calvin William Gutelius, living at Northumberland, Pa.

Mary Martha Gutelius, drowned in 1856.

Emma Jane Gutelius. living with Mrs. Reuben Coles, Philadelphia. Pa.

Henry Clay Gutelius. Deceased.

Mrs. Clara Gutelius Bechtle living at East Greenville, Pa.

Mrs. Florence Gutelius Coles. living in Philadelphia. Pa.

ANNIE MARIA GUTELIUS.

Tenth child and third daughter of Frederick A. and Anna Catherine Bistel Gutelius, was born March 17th, 1805 and died April 4th, 1805, age 17 days.

HENRY GUTELIUS.

Eleventh child and eighth son of Frederick A. and Anna Catherine Bistel Gutelius, was born in Mifflinburg. Pennsylvania May 27th, 1806, and died March 3rd, 1876, age 69 years. 9 months and 6 days. He was a hatter by trade. He was united in marriage to Catherine Musser, March 29th, 1829. Her death occurred May 19th, 1882.

Born to this union, ten children:

John Frederick Gutelius, born February 21st, 1830 and died April ————, 1883.

Catherine Elizabeth Gutelius, born March 28th, 1831. died February 27th, 1832.

Samuel Andrew Gutelius, born December 5th, 1832, died in 1911.

Maria C. Gutelius, born July 28th, 1834, died June 23rd, 1873.

Sarah Jane Gutelius, born October 9th 1836, died August 2nd, 1912.

Anna Catherine Gutelius, born February 20th, 1839, died June 18th, 1840.

Emma Jane Gutelius Shaffner, born February 23rd, 1841. Address Carlisle, Pa.

Lydia Ann Gutelius Maus, born October 19th, 1842. Address, Frizellburg, Md.

Ellen Louisa Gutelius, born December 11th, 1845. Address Harrisburg Pa.

Catherine Isabella Gutelius, born February 12th, 1849, died September 14th, 1907.

ANDREW GUTELIUS.

Twelfth child and eighth son of Frederick A. and Anna Catherine Bistel Gutelius, was born at Mifflinburg, Pa., April 16th, 1808, died September 5th, 1874, age 66 years. 4 months and 19 days. He was united in marriage to Lydia Fisher, who was born November 2nd, 1811 and died July 4th, 1853.

They always lived in Mifflinburg and are buried there.

Born to this union, four children:

Fisher Gutelius, born July 17th, 1844, died July 30th, 1906.

Mary E. Gutelius, born October 19th, 1847, died March 13th, 1852.

Hannah Gutelius Romig, born August 18th, 1848, died January 8th, 1911.

Amanda E Gutelius Williamson, born July 18th, 1850. Address Hebron, Neb.

Andrew's education was attained mostly by attending German School. Was a cabinet maker by trade in early life, then entered mercantile business and in later years took contracts for building houses.

He was a Christian man, faithfully performing his duties to his motherless children and never remarried. At his death he was a member of the Presbyterian Church.

His only son, Rev. Fisher Gutelius, was educated for the ministry at the Union Theological Seminary in New York City and became pastor of the Presbyterian Church at Moscow, N. Y., which pulpit he held for 32 years. He served in the Civil War, belonging to Company D, 150th Pennsylvania Regiment.

His widow, Mrs. Francis Gutelius, is still living. They were the parents of four children:

Stanley Fisher Gutelius, was born May 31st, 1879. He is pastor of Union Congregation Church at Kobe, Japan.

Helen Gutelius Strobel, born October 24th 1881.

Benjamin Stuart Gutelius, born November 27th, 1885.

Henry Kieffer Gutelius, born August 6th, 1889.

Mrs. Amanda Gutelius Williamson's youngest son, Harry Gutelius Romig, is a missionary under the Foreign Missionary board of the Presbyterian Church at Tenghsien, Shantung, Province, China.

SARAH (SALLY) GUTELIUS.

Thirteenth child and fourth daughter of Frederick A. and Anna Catherine Bistel Gutelius, was born in Mifflinburg, Pennsylvania, January 4th, 1811 and died April 29th, 1893, age 82 years 3 months and 25 days, she being the last of a family of eleven brothers and four sisters to pass to the great beyond. She was united in marriage to Samuel Grove, who was born in New Berlin, Pennsylvania, in 1798 and died in 1873. They were members of the Reformed Church and are buried at Mifflinburg, Pa.

Born to this union, three children:

Anna Maria Grove Lucas, born January, 1842, living in Chicago, Ill.

Sarah Catherine Grove Hoffman, born in 1843, died 1909.

Samuel Gutelius Grove, born in 1845, living in Mifflinburg, Pa.

GEORGE GUTELIUS.

Fourteenth child and tenth son of Frederick A. and Anna Catherine Distel Gutelius was born November 1st, 1812, in Mifflinburg, Pa. Died April 27th, 1889, age 76 years, 5 months and 26 days, having always lived at Mifflinburg. He was united in marriage to Catherine Sophia Alspach, September 18th, 1834. Her death occurred July 14th, 1892.

At an early age he learned the cabinet trade, then engaged in the foundry business until after the Civil War, when he retired He had some land and he farmed it until his death. He was a member of the Reformed Church.

Born to this union, nine children:

Elmira Elizabeth Gutelius Millet, born July 26th, 1835. Died in February, 1885. Was married to John K. Millet, July 5th, 1859. To this union, five children were born.

George Calvin Gutelius was born January 25th, 1838. Died May 18th, 1919. Was married to Amelia Malinda Beaver, March 15th, 1866. To this union five children were born.

Henry Edwin Gutelius was born January 4th, 1840. Died September 10th, 1912 Was married to Caroline Rishel in 1868. To this union seven children were born.

Anna Catherine Gutelius Housil was born December 9th, 1841. Died in 1884, in Missouri. Was married to David Housil. No children were born to this union.

Susan Armetia Gutelius Hursh was born February 1st, 1844. Died December 24th, 1912. Was married to William Hursh in June, 1863. To this union nine children were born.

Martha Jane Gutelius Kleckner was born February

14th, 1846. Was married to George O. Kleckner November 19th, 1863. To this union ten children were born. Mr. and Mrs Kleckner are still living at Mifflinburg, Pa.

Mary Ellen Gutelius Zimmerman, was born March 23rd, 1848. Was married to Samuel Zimmerman July 14th, 1867, whose death occurred October 5th, 1877. To this union seven children were born. Mrs. Zimmerman is still living at Mifflinburg, Pa.

Ada Valeria Gutelius Rishel Henry was born September 21st, 1850. Was married to John Rishel, September 21st, 1869, whose death occurred in 1879. To this union five children were born. She then married Josiah Henry. She is still living, address Milwaukee, Wis.

John Theodore Gutelius was born December 28th, 1853. Was married to Ida Dye, in September, 1878, who died, March 15th, 1881. To this union two children were born. He married a second time and he and his wife are living at Centralia, Iowa.

JOSEPH GUTELIUS.

Youngest, fifteenth child, eleventh son, of Frederick A. and Anna Catherine Bistel Gutelius, was born at Mifflinburg, Pa., November 4th, 1815, died February 10th, 1866, age 50 years, 3 months and 6 days. He was killed by being struck on the head by a falling tree. Was married to Elizabeth Garrett, January 25th, 1844. She was born March 24th, 1818 and died January 29th, 1892. His occupation was that of a carpenter. Was a member of the Reformed Church.

Born to this union, five children:

William Howard Gutelius, born April 10th 1845, and died August 31st, 1872. Unmarried and had just completed his education preparatory to entering the ministry. Died at Lancaster, Pa., at the seminary.

Ada Eleanor Gutelius, born August 2nd, 1847, died October 14th, 1847.

Albert S. Gutelius, born October 24th, 1848. He resides

in the old homestead of his Grandfather. Frederick A. Gutelius, in Mifflinburg, Pa. He has three children.

Elliott J. Gutelius, born October 30th, 1851. In the grocery business at Mifflinburg, Pa. He is the father of two sons and one daughter.

Oliva Gutelius, born August 13th, 1858. Was married to A. A. Hopp. They reside at Mifflinburg. They are parents of four children, two of whom are living.

DESCENDANTS OF
JOHN PETER GUTELIUS
AND
(MARIA ARNDT GUTELIUS)
(HENRIETTA TURNER GUTELIUS)

SUSAN CATHERINE GUTELIUS.

Daughter of John Peter and Maria Arndt Gutelius, was born November 4th, 1828, died —————————,1897. Was married to Theodore Frantz.

Born to this union, nine children:
Gertrude Frantz
Daniel Frantz.
Arndt Frantz.
William Frantz.
Charles Frantz.
Edward Frantz.
—————— Frantz.
—————— Frantz.
—————— Frantz.

MARGARET ARNDT GUTELIUS.

Daughter of John Peter and Maria Arndt Gutelius, was born December 18th, 1832, died May 4th, 1905. Was united in marriage to Lr. J. R. McCleery who was born October 22nd, 1825 and died April 21st 1874. Both buried in Fairview Cemetery at Bluffton, Indiana.

Born to this union, nine children:

Maria Elizabeth Huff, born August 20th, 1850. Address, Mendon, Mich.

John Gutelius McCleery, born July 5th, 1852. Address, Bluffton, Indiana.

Susan Catherine North, born February 23rd, 1854. Address, Bluffton, Indiana.

Ida Jane Altdoeffer, born August 2nd 1856.

Mary Alice Stine, born November 22nd, 1859. Address, Bryan, Ohio.

Cora Margaret Van Gorder, born November 2nd, 1862. Address, South Bend, Ind.

Anna Augusta Bennett, born May 16th, 1865. Address, Ridgeway. N. J

Lulu Maud McCleery, born April 5th, 1868. Deceased.

James Ross McCleery, born June 16th, 1871. Deceased.

1702692

MARTHA JANE GUTELIUS.

Daughter of John Peter and Henrietta Turner Gutelius was born at Mifflinburg, Pa., January 13th, 1840. Was united in marriage to Robert Y. Saylor, in 1858, whose death occurred in 1905. Mrs. Saylor's address is Marion, Indiana.

Born to this union, two children:

Maude Eve Saylor, born September 20th, 1862, died April 16th, 1906.

Frank Gutelius Saylor, born February 2nd, 1867.

Frank G. Saylor was married to Mary Louise Wiggins, July 8th, 1891. He is a traveling salesman, address, Indianapolis, Indiana.

Born to this union:

Lucile Saylor, December 12th, 1892.

HENRIETTA L. GUTELIUS.

Was born at Homer, Ohio, April 8th, 1843. Was united in marriage to Marcellus M. Justus, July 2nd, 1876. Mr. Justus was Sheriff of Wells County for four years and served two terms, 1913 and 1915, as a member of the House of Representatives of Indiana. Served in the 88th Indiana Infantry during the Civil War. Address, Bluffton, Indiana.

They are parents of four children:

Myrtle Justus.

Lewis C. Justus, deceased, killed in Kingsland interurban wreck, September 21, 1910.

Morton Justus.

Agnes Justus.

Myrtle Justus, was united in marriage to Albert M. Forst, January 16th, 1900. Address, Bluffton, Indiana.

Lewis C. Justus, was united in marriage to Jennie North, October 4th, 1896. Born to this union:

Lewis Justus, February 24th, 1902.

Morton Justus, was united in marriage to Clementine

Birch. Address. Tucumcari, New Mex. Born to this union:

      Guy McBride Justus.
      Marcellus Justus.
      Mary Ellen Justus.

Agnes Justus, was united in marriage to Harry Webber Address, St. Louis, Mo. Born to this union:

      Justus Webber.

WILLIAM ALLEN GUTELIUS.

Son of John Peter and Henrietta Turner Gutelius, was born at Pickerington, Ohio, June 5th, 1848. He was united in marriage to Mary Francis Buckles, at Fort Wayne Indiana, June 21st, 1871. Still engaged in the drug business in Bluffton, Indiana. He was Postmaster of Bluffton, Indiana during President Grover Cleveland's second administration. Mrs. Gutelius died February 20th, 1916.

Born to this union, six children:

Will B. Gutelius, born May 10th, 1872.

Harry E. Gutelius, born September 21st, 1873.

Harriet L. Gutelius, born December 13th, 1875.

Nettie Gutelius, born April 13th, 1877.

Maude E. Gutelius, born July 19th, 1879.

Mary Gutelius, born August 13th, 1885.

Will Buckles Gutelius, was married to Mae Snedden May 31st, 1894. Manufacturer of Handles. Address Bluffton Indiana. 32 Degree Mason and Shriner.

Harry E. Gutelius, was married to Maude Miller, September 23rd, 1896. Merchant, Kendallville, Indiana.

Born to this union, four children:

      Kathryn Louise Gutelius, born July 30th, 1898.
      Martha Lucile Gutelius, born February 1st, 1902
      Maude Gutelius, born September 27th, 1906.
      Mary Jane Gutelius, born January 29th, 1916.

Harriet L. Gutelius, was married to Harry A. Gable June 9th, 1903. Manufacturer. Marion, Indiana. Knight Templar, 32 Degree Mason and Shriner.

Nettie Gutelius, unmarried, address Bluffton, Indiana.

Maude E. Gutelius, was married to Frank I. Louis;'.., October 17th, 1900. Manager National Supply Co., Tulsa, Okla. Knight Templar and Shriner.

Mary Gutelius, was married to Paul T. Williams, January 16th, 1905. Salesman National Supply Co., Independence, Kansas.

Born to this union:

Paul Gutelius Williams, born August 7th, 1909.

EMMA MARIA GUTELIUS.

Daughter of John Peter and Henrietta Turner Gutelius was born Carroll, Ohio, January 17th, 1852. Was united in marriage to Joseph S. Dailey, March 15th, 1870. Mr. Dailey was Judge of the Wells and Huntington Circuit Court for 12 years and a member of the Supreme Court of the State of Indiana. Mr. Dailey died, October 9th, 1905. Mrs. Dailey's address, is Bluffton, Ind.

Born to this union, four children:

Frank Coffroth Dailey, born December 22nd, 1870.

Lewis Warrington Dailey, born March 8th, 1874.

Charles Gutelius Dailey, born March 29th, 1876.

Blanche Dailey, born February 9th, 1886.

Frank C. Dailey, was married to Edna Field, October 17th, 1894.

Born to this union, three children:

Field Tribolet Dailey, born August 3rd, 1895.

Joseph Leonard Dailey, born August 28th, 1896.

George Simmons Dailey, born June 16th, 1903.

Mr. Dailey was appointed United States District Attorney for Indiana, by President Woodrow Wilson. Address, Indianapolis, Indiana. 32 Degree Mason and Shriner.

Lewis W. Dailey, was married to Lizzie Rogers, June 22nd. 1893. Dentist, Bluffton, Indiana. 32 Degree Mason.

Born to this union, four children:

Josephine Dailey, born December 22nd, 1894 died March 19th, 1905.

Elizabeth Dailey, born January 21st, 1897.
Roger L. Dailey, born November 9th, 1899.
James S. Dailey, born July 15th, 1906.
Charles G. Dailey, was married to Daisy Miller. June 20th, 1899. Member of firm of Simmons & Dailey, Attorneys, Bluffton Indiana. 32 Degree Mason.
Born to this union,
Robert M. Dailey, born August 5th, 1904.
Blanche Dailey, unmarried. Address Bluffton, Ind.

THOMAS HOLMES GUTELIUS.

Originally named Frank Nelson Gutelius, was born at Carroll, Ohio, May 8th, 1856. Traveling salesman, Indianapolis, Indiana.
He was married to Gertrude Smith, June 7th, 1877.
Born to this union, six children:
Charles Bradford Gutelius, June 19th, 1878.
Earl Gutelius.
Gene Gutelius.
Harry Brooks Gutelius, December 16th, 1882.
Margaret Bowes Gutelius, October 12th, 1886.
Gertrude Gutelius, May 17th, 1892.
Dr. Charles Bradford Gutelius, Physician, unmarried, Indianapolis, Indiana.
Harry Brooks Gutelius with Jones Bros. Oil Co., Tulsa, Okla. Married to Ethel Bonge, April 20th, 1910.
Born to this union, two children:
Thomas Holmes Gutelius, February 15th 1911.
Margaret Jane Gutelius, February 5th, 1913.
Margaret Gutelius. married to Clarence Joel Pearson, October 20th. 1910. Indianapolis, Indiana.
Gertrude Gutelius, unmarried, Indianapolis, Indiana.